SMART ABOUT
History

Valley of the
Golden
Mummies

Toilet paper is a do-it-yourself mummy kit.

But it doesn't last!

By Dan Digz

Written and illustrated by Joan Holub

Grosset & Dunlap • New York

For Jane O'Connor and Monique Stephens,
two golden editors—J.H.

And with thanks to Holland Gallagher, a model child

Photo Credits:
Cover, pp. 6, 7, 12, 13, 14, 15, 16, 18, 20, 30 © Kenneth Garrett; pp. 1, 5 © Kathleen Parry; p. 8 © Scala / Art Resource, NY; p. 9 © Mary Evans Picture Library; p. 11 © Joan Holub; p. 23 from *Fun with Hieroglyphs* by Catharine Roehrig, copyright © 1990 by The Metropolitan Museum of Art. Used by permission of Viking Penguin, an imprint of Penguin Putnam Books for Young Readers, a division of Penguin Putnam Inc.; p. 25 (left) Universal Studios / courtesy of Everett Collection; p. 25 (insert) Everett Collection; p. 26 © Robert Harding Picture Library; p. 27 © C M Dixon; p. 32 © Erich Lessing / Art Resource, NY

Library of Congress Cataloging in Publication Data is available.

ISBN 0-448-42661-7 (pbk)   A B C D E F G H I J
ISBN 0-448-42817-2 (GB)   A B C D E F G H I J

From the desk of
Ms. Brandt

Dear Class,
   We have been learning about so many exciting events from the past. Now you may choose a subject that is of special interest to you for your report.
   You may write about something that happened thousands of years ago or about something that happened not so very long ago - maybe when your parents or your grandparents were your age. It's up to you!

   Here are some questions you might want to think about:

🍎 What made you pick your topic?

🍎 Did you learn anything that really surprised you?

   Good luck and have fun!
                          Ms. Brandt

Why I am writing about mummies:

I am writing my history report about mummies for three reasons:

Reason 1   One time on vacation, I saw a mummy in the Metropolitan Museum of Art in New York City. It was old and creepy, but it was interesting, too. I have liked mummies ever since then.

Reason 2   I broke my arm playing soccer. Now it is in a cast. The doctor wrapped it in cloth that gets hard. That is kind of like what happens with a mummy.

Reason 3   Since I couldn't play soccer with a broken arm, I watched TV instead. I saw a TV show about Egyptian mummies.

So when my teacher (Hi, Ms. Brandt!) told us to write a report, I thought of three things to write about: 1. Mummies 2. Mummies 3. More mummies!

This is how ancient Egyptians wrote numbers. This is page number 4.

‖

Striking Gold

The green part is Egypt.

AFRICA

I used to think all the mummies in Egypt were found a long, long time ago. Surprise! Lots more mummies were found just a few years ago. It happened by accident. On March 1, 1996, a man was riding his donkey through the Egyptian desert. The donkey stumbled into a hole. The man hopped off his donkey and looked into the hole. There was a golden mummy face peeking back at him from under the sand. He had struck gold—mummy gold!

Hey, Look!

This is just one of the tombs in the Valley of the Golden Mummies in Bahariya, Egypt.

Mummy Hunters

Archeologists like me study how people lived long, long, long ago.

The man told archeologists about the golden mummy. They rushed into the desert. When they started digging, they found more golden mummies. Soon everybody started calling the place the Valley of the Golden Mummies. (That is such a cool name.)

Archeologists spend a lot of time cleaning mummies in the Valley of the Golden Mummies.

Archeologists were excited to find the mummies. The golden mummies had been buried about 2,330 years ago. Luckily, their tombs had never been robbed in all the time since then. Most other Egyptian tombs were robbed way back in ancient times.

What is a MUMMY?

The mummy of Egyptian Pharaoh Ramesses II looks like it is going to grab someone.

A mummy is a dead body that gets dried out so it won't rot. Bacteria make dead things rot. Bodies are about two-thirds water. Bacteria like to grow in wet places, but if a dead body gets dried out, bacteria can't grow. A dried-out body can stay almost the same for thousands of years.

Stuff that rhymes with mummy:

 yummy

 mommy (sort of)

 Gummi

 tummy

All wrapped up with some place to go

Why did ancient Egyptians make mummies, anyway? It was an icky job that took a lot of time. I read lots of books and here is what I learned:

The ancient Egyptians believed there was life after death—an afterlife! In the afterlife, the spirit of the dead person could still enjoy all kinds of things, like eating, playing games, and going on boat rides.

But to do all this, the spirit needed its body. And a rotten body wouldn't do. That's why the Egyptians took so much time turning a dead body into a mummy—to keep it in good shape for the afterlife.

A mummy headed for the afterlife in a sort of sled-boat.

What's inside a mummy's tummy?

It took ancient Egyptians seventy days to make a mummy. Here's how they did it:

First, the wet, slimy "guts" were taken out. The intestines, stomach, liver, and lungs were each put in a special jar. Egyptians believed that people thought with their hearts, so the heart was left in the body.

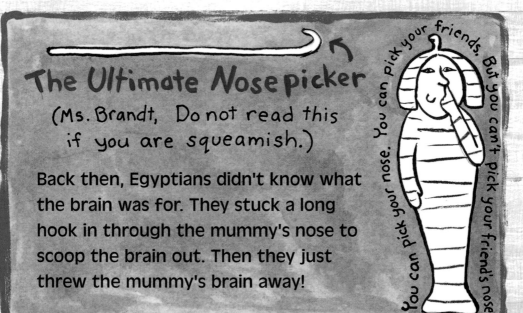

The Ultimate Nose picker

(Ms. Brandt, Do not read this if you are squeamish.)

Back then, Egyptians didn't know what the brain was for. They stuck a long hook in through the mummy's nose to scoop the brain out. Then they just threw the mummy's brain away!

Don't try this at home!

You can pick your nose. You can pick your friends. But you can't pick your friend's nose.

Next, the body was covered in a special salt. It was called natron. Salt helps soak up wet stuff. After forty days, the salt was cleaned off. The body looked dry and shrively now.

←This means 10.

Oil, tree sap, and wax were put on the body.
This was to keep the body from getting wet again.
The body was stuffed with sawdust or cloth to
keep its shape. Then the body was wrapped with
strips of cloth. The strips went around and around
the body like the bandages on my cast.
The Egyptians put good-luck charms called
amulets between the cloth strips. Now the
mummy was done. It was put in a coffin and
was supposed to stay in its tomb forever.

an
amulet
↓

Before
↓

Salt

Mummy
in Progress

I made a tomato mummy.
Here's how to do it:
Pour one inch of salt into a bowl.
Ask a grown-up to cut a tomato in half.
Wash out the wet part.
Put the tomatoes on top of the salt.
Add salt until they are covered up.
Wait 30 days.
Dig up the tomatoes.
Voila! Tomato mummies!

←After

Don't worry, Ms. Brandt, I'm not going to eat them!

Mummy ABCs

Archeologists think there may be 10,000 mummies in the Valley of the Golden Mummies. So far, they have found more than one hundred. They have a long way to go to find all of them!

No one knows the names of the mummies. So archeologists gave them nicknames like Mr. X, the Bride, Mummy A, Mummy B, and Mummy C.

This is smiling Mummy B. →

The archeologists believe Mummy B was the wife of Mummy A. They think this because her head is turned so she seems to be looking at Mummy A.

Stop staring, dear.

They also found two child mummies in the valley. They nicknamed them the boy mummy and the girl mummy. (I think they could have come up with better names than that.)

Oh boy! It's a boy mummy.

This is the girl mummy. It looks like someone is painting her, but they are really cleaning her with a brush.

Mummy B and the girl mummy are smiling. Not very many other smiling mummies have ever been found. I think their smiles look spooky, as if they have a secret they aren't telling.

Giftwrapped in Gold

Not all of the mummies found in the valley had gold on them. Only rich people could afford that. The archeologists found three main kinds of mummies in the Valley of the Golden Mummies:

Poor and Not-so-Poor Mummies

Mummies of poor people were wrapped in cloth strips any old way. Mummies of people with a little money were carefully wrapped in cloth strips. The strips were crisscrossed to make patterns and designs. Mr. X is this kind of mummy.

I think Mr. X got his name because scientists X-rayed him to study him.

Kind-of-Rich Mummies

Mummies of people with more money wore colorful painted masks on their face and chest. The masks were made of cloth dipped in plaster to make it stiff and hard. Mummy C is this kind of mummy.

There is a picture of Mummy C on the cover of my report.

Rich Mummies

The richest mummies got masks painted with bright colors, too. Their masks were also painted with real gold! Some of the gold had jewels and carved pictures on it. The masks weren't solid gold. Only the kings (pharaohs) were rich enough for that. But the masks still cost a lot. Mummies A and B are this kind of mummy.

Mummy A was a rich man.

Mummies Take a Trip

When people heard about the Valley of the Golden Mummies, everyone wanted to visit. Archeologists worried that if too many people came, they might get in the way of the work. So they sent Mummies A, B, and C, and the boy and girl mummies to a museum a few hours away. Then people could go to the museum to see the mummies and not bother the archeologists.

← The girl mummy gets packed up for her trip to the museum.

This way to the museum →

A Mummy Curse?

After the mummies left, one of the archeologists began having bad dreams. He dreamed about the boy and girl mummies, who were at the museum. The boy and girl had been found next to each other in the Valley of the Golden Mummies, so they were probably brother and sister. A male mummy was next to them, too. He was probably their dad. The dad stayed behind at the tomb. The archeologist wondered if maybe the girl and boy mummies missed the dad mummy after they went to the museum.

The archeologist sent the dad mummy to the museum to be with the boy and girl mummies—just in case! Guess what! The archeologist's bad dreams stopped! Had his dreams been part of a mummy curse?

More Mummy Curses

This is King Tut. He is the most famous mummy ever!

King Tut's face mask is solid gold. It must be worth a gazillion dollars.

The idea of mummy curses began after the mummy of King Tutankhamen was found. His name was too long and too hard to say. That's why he got the nickname King Tut. (I have a nickname, too. Dan is shorter than my real name—Daniel.) King Tut's tomb was found in Egypt in 1922. It was full of golden treasure. That was the good news.

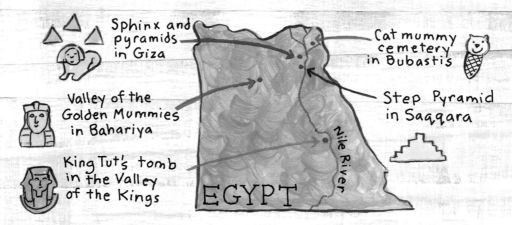

Sphinx and pyramids in Giza

Cat mummy cemetery in Bubastis

Valley of the Golden Mummies in Bahariya

Step Pyramid in Saqqara

King Tut's tomb in the Valley of the Kings

Nile River

EGYPT

The bad news was that some of the people working on the tomb had bad luck or died. It could be that old germs in the tomb made them sick. That's why archeologists wear masks in tombs nowadays.

But back then, people believed in the curse of King Tut. They thought he was mad because stuff was being taken from his tomb. Maybe he was getting even! The weird thing is that lots of tombs really do have curses written on them. Ancient Egyptians wrote the curses to scare off robbers.

A curse like this was written on the door of an old Egyptian tomb:

Forget it! I'm not going to rob a tomb with a curse.

Egyptian kings were called pharaohs.

"They that shall break the seal of Pharaoh's tomb shall meet death by a disease that no doctor can diagnose."

A Mummy Moves In

Rich Egyptians wanted their mummies to have everything they needed in the afterlife, so they put things like furniture, games, money, and food in the tombs. They put in little statues of servants, too. The servants were supposed to work for the mummies in the afterlife.

These things were in the golden mummies' tombs:

a picture of some Egyptian gods

pots for water so mummy would not get thirsty

glass bottles for wine or make-up

mummy money

a painted mummy mask

This means 20.

Stuff I would take if I were a mummy:

Rock collection

LAST FOREVER
JELLYBEANS
GIANT SIZE

Jellybeans

MY soccer ball

Telephone

COOL COMIC BOOK

Comic books

Computer games

Scooter

Mummy Dearest

Egyptians tried to make it easy for each spirit to find the right mummy in the afterlife. They put a face mask on each mummy that looked like the person when the person was alive. And they wrote the person's name on the mummy or on the tomb walls.

Egyptian writing was called hieroglyphics. Hieroglyphs look like little pictures of animals and objects. They can be written left to right, right to left, or top to bottom in a column. I'm glad we don't write like that. It would make reading hard!

This is the hieroglyphic alphabet:

A cake	A bat	B body	C K cat kite	CH checkers
D dig	E eat honey	E pet	F fork	G gold
H help	I sit kite	J jelly	L lemon	M mask
N nose	O open foot	P pyramid	Q queen	R rich
S soccer	SH ship	T tomb	TH bath	U mummy
V valley	W wow	X box	Y yes	Z zoo

Guess what this spells:

Answer: (my name) DAN DIGZ

Mummy Madness

People didn't just take the stuff in mummies' tombs. They took the mummies, too! In the 1800s, a man in England sold tickets to shows where he unwrapped mummies from Egypt. He called the shows "mummy unrollings." One time, someone sold him a fake mummy. When he unwrapped the bandages during his show, all he found was lots of trash!

© North Wind Picture Archives

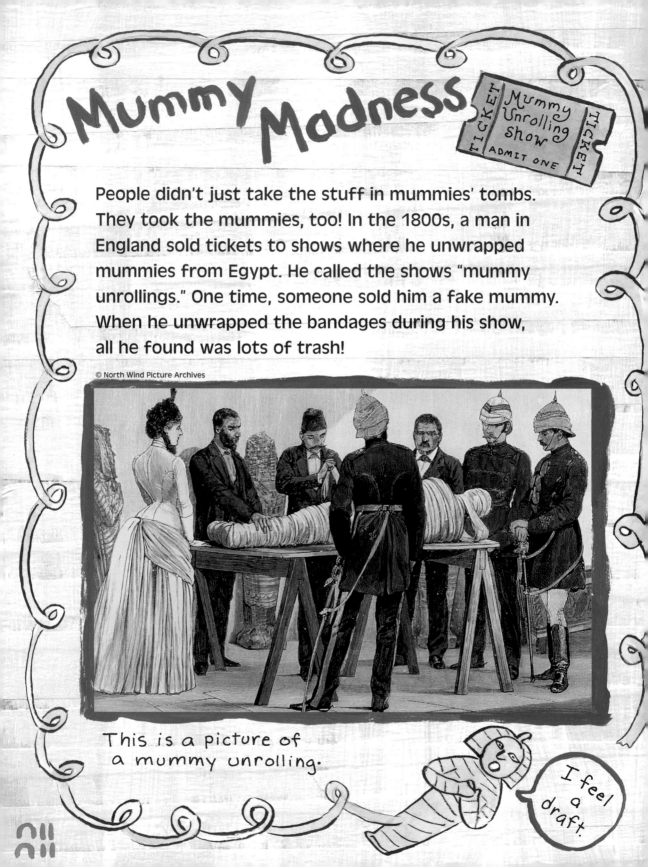

This is a picture of a mummy unrolling.

I feel a draft.

Mummy Movies

This poster is → from the 1932 movie, _The Mummy._ Looks spooky!

← This _cool_ poster is from the 1999 movie, _The Mummy._

The first long movies were made just about the time that King Tut was discovered. So someone made a scary movie called _The Mummy_ in 1932.

New movies called _The Mummy_ and _The Mummy Returns_ were made just a few years ago. People still love mummies!

Can you read my secret coded message? →

Lots O' Mummies

The mummies in Egypt were made on purpose. But sometimes, a dead body gets turned into a mummy by accident. That happens when it gets buried in stuff that keeps it from rotting. Mummies have been found in bogs, ice, and deserts all over the world.

Bogs are deep swamps filled with cold water. Bog water doesn't have bacteria, so things don't rot in it. One famous bog mummy is called Tollund Man because he was found in Tollund Bog in Denmark. The man died 2,400 years ago, but his mummy is in such good shape that you can still see his whiskers!

This is Tollund Man, a mummy who needs a shave.

← weird with a beard!

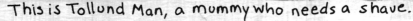

Cat Mummies

People weren't the only ones made into mummies in ancient Egypt. Egyptians loved animals—especially cats. They even worshipped a cat goddess named Bastet. When a pet cat died, they usually made it into a mummy.

← A 3,000-year-old Egyptian cat mummy wrapped in cloth strips.

Mummy Wrap-Up

It may take fifty years or longer to find all the mummies in the Valley of the Golden Mummies. A man named Dr. Zahi Hawass is the director of the archeologists in the valley. He has a website with lots of information about the golden mummies at http://www.guardians.net/hawass/

People can go to the Bahariya Museum in Egypt to see the golden mummies. But you don't have to go all the way to Egypt to see a mummy. You can see one at the Metropolitan Museum of Art in New York City like I did. A museum in Chicago, Illinois, called the Field Museum, has mummies, too.

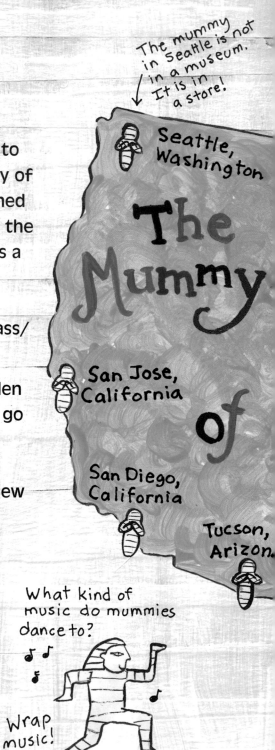

The mummy in Seattle is not in a museum. It is in a store!

The Mummy of

Seattle, Washington

San Jose, California

San Diego, California

Tucson, Arizona

A moomy!

What would you get if you crossed a mummy and a cow?

Why won't mummies watch scary movies?

Because they don't have the guts.

What kind of music do mummies dance to?

Wrap music!

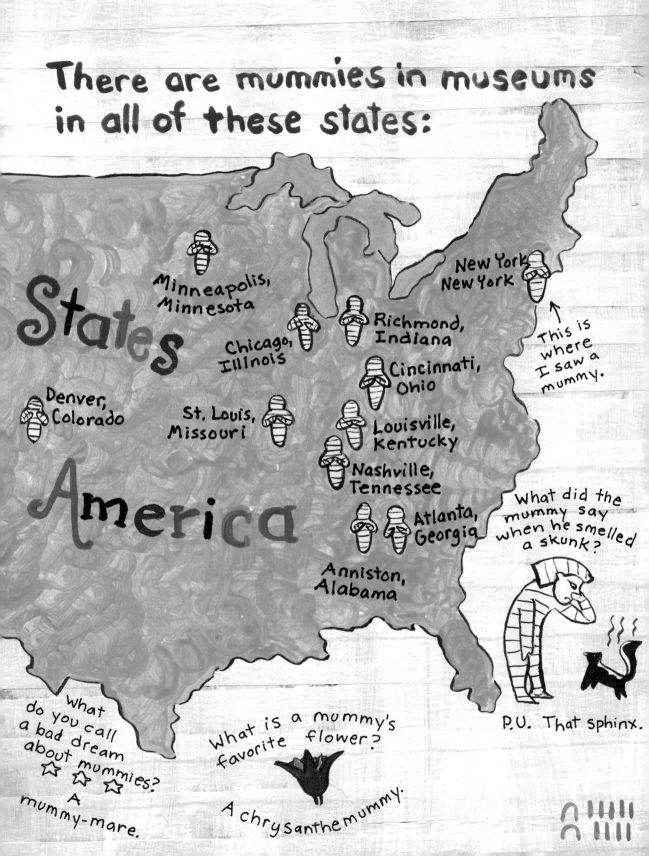

There are mummies in museums in all of these states:

States

America

Minneapolis, Minnesota

New York, New York

This is where I saw a mummy.

Chicago, Illinois

Richmond, Indiana

Denver, Colorado

Cincinnati, Ohio

St. Louis, Missouri

Louisville, Kentucky

Nashville, Tennessee

What did the mummy say when he smelled a skunk?

Atlanta, Georgia

Anniston, Alabama

P.U. That sphinx.

What do you call a bad dream about mummies? A mummy-mare.

What is a mummy's favorite flower? A chrysanthemummy.

These are surprising

1 Egyptians paid women to cry and act sad at their funerals. The women hadn't even known the dead person. Weird!

These statues of crying women were in the golden mummies' tombs. I wonder how much money women got paid to cry?

2 Ancient Egyptians had lots of tooth trouble. Sometimes they even went to the dentist to get their teeth fixed. When scientists x-rayed Mr. X, they found out that two of his teeth had been pulled.

3 By 500 A.D., the Egyptians had made 70 million mummies! Then their religion changed. They didn't believe in mummies anymore. So they stopped making them.

This means 30.

things I learned about mummies:

4 Some people don't think mummies should be dug up. I know I wouldn't like it if somebody dug me up after I died! I wouldn't want to be in a museum, either. But the only way most people can get to see a mummy Is in a museum, so I'm glad some mummies are dug up.

Here's How I Made the Pages in My Report Look Like Mummy Pages:

I stuck long pieces of tape on sheets of cardboard to make each page. Then I swished white paint over the tape. Since I wanted it to look old like a mummy, I didn't have to be neat. I printed some of my report on the computer and pasted it on top of the tape. I wrote some of the words with a marker or with paint.

cardboard

←Tape

Paint

Words I Learned:

Amulet - a good-luck charm to keep bad spirits away.

Canopic Jars - special jars that ancient Egyptians used to hold a mummy's intestines, stomach, liver, and lungs.

Stomach goes in here.

Liver goes in here.

Intestines go in here.

Lungs go in here.

Cartonnage - a hard covering over a mummy's face and chest, made of plaster and cloth.

Hieroglyphics - ancient Egyptian writing, which uses pictures instead of letters.

Dan, you did a great job! I am a mummy maniac, too. You might like to read _Mummies_ by Joyce Milton and _Cat Mummies_ by Kelly Trumble — two good mummy books.

Ms. Brandt